D1187438

Camels
and
Llamas

written and illustrated by

Olive L. Earle

WILLIAM MORROW AND COMPANY   NEW YORK   1961

In long-past ages, when huge prehistoric animals roamed the earth, the ancestors of today's camels and llamas lived in North America. Fossils have been found which prove that they lived here more than forty million years ago. At that time they were no bigger than hares. During the thousands and thousands of years that went by, the little animals developed in size, just as the eohippus — the tiny prehistoric horse — evolved into the horse of today.

As generation followed generation, and the small forebears of the camel family became bigger and bigger, the extent of their range widened. They spread out until some of them finally reached Asia by way of the land bridge that once connected Alaska and the Old World. These were the original ancestors of today's camels. Others journeyed to South America, where they now form the llama group. Here in North America the camel family became extinct.

In Asia, the one-humped camels disap-

peared as wild animals but survived as domestic animals, in areas where the climate was suitably warm and dry. It is known that they became the slaves of man at least five thousand years ago, and records show that they were introduced into Egypt from Arabia some thousand years later. In the Bible, six thousand camels are listed as part of Job's wealth, and there are many other references to camels, as well as dromedaries.

In Central Asia two-humped camels are still found in wild herds. But opinions differ as to whether they are truly wild or whether they are feral; that is, the descendants of once tame animals which long ago escaped from their owners. The so-called wild horses of our West are feral animals, for they are mostly the descendants of horses brought here and abandoned long ago by early Spanish explorers.

All camels have the same general outline, except for the hump. The Arabian camel, as he is generally known, has only one hump, while the Bactrian camel, more commonly used in Asia, has two humps.

Camels—both Arabian and Bactrian—belong to the ruminant, or cud-chewing group of animals. Ruminants swallow food which has been partly chewed and later, somewhat softened by digestive juices, is brought up to the mouth again as a cud, for further chewing. Oxen and sheep are among the many animals that chew the cud. The giraffe is also a ruminant, and perhaps this habit, as well as his spots, earned him his early name, "cameleopard."

A ruminant chews its food with a side-to-side movement of the lower jaw instead of the up-and-down action that we use.

Typical ruminants, such as the cow, have four distinct compartments in the stomach for their complicated digestive process. The camel's stomach also has four, but the divisions are imperfect and it is generally said that there are only three distinct chambers. In the walls of part of the stomach there are pouches that can be opened or closed by means of muscles which surround them. The exact purpose of these pouches is not definitely known. They were once thought to be water reservoirs, but it is now believed that the liquid that may be in them is, in some way, an aid to the digestion of dry food.

There are many recognized varieties of the one-humped, or Arabian camel. These differing breeds may be roughly divided into two groups: baggage camels; and riding camels, or dromedaries. The name *dromedary* means running camel. It is also sometimes called *mehari*. Often *dromedary* is the name used for all Arabian, or one-humped camels.

For centuries baggage camels have been famous for their ability to carry loads across the desert sands. Though once they were the only means of transport in the Sahara and in deserts of the Middle East, nowadays there are also airplanes and motor vehicles in many regions. But even today the camel often makes better headway on a sandy road than a truck does.

Not so long ago, great companies of as many as twenty thousand baggage camels loaded with merchandise set out, with their

attendants, to cross the Sahara—the desert region of North Africa. Camel caravans, as they are called, though smaller today, are still used by traders. Usually the camels travel one after the other, and caravans may string along for miles, like some huge crawling snake. The drivers keep them moving by beating, punching, or shouting at them. They also urge them on by means of singing and flute playing, for camels are supposed to respond to music.

The baggage camel, like his relatives, is noted for his ability to go without water. When none is available, he can travel for three or four days without quenching his thirst. Some camels are able to live without water for ten days or even longer. These camels may have been trained to go long periods without drinking. The need for water depends, in part, on the amount of work done and on the season of the year. In the extreme dry heat of summer the camel needs more water than in winter, when he gets moisture from green plants. Given the opportunity, he will drink from five to seven gallons a day. A very thirsty camel has been known to die from drinking too much.

It is probably the camel's acute sense of smell that makes him aware of water in a desert oasis while he is still miles away from it. It is also thought that he remembers a watering spot, once he has visited it.

A well-cared-for camel is fed on dates, grain, and green fodder, but on the march he sometimes has to live on dried leaves, seeds, pods, and the branches of whatever desert plants he can find. The membrane on the inside of his mouth and on his tongue is so tough that the spines of the thorniest plants cannot penetrate it. Driven by hunger, he will eat straw matting, baskets, or anything else near the rest camp that he finds edible. Sometimes at the end of a long day's journey camels are hobbled; that is, their feet are tied. But even then they manage to move around a little to forage.

Like other camels, the baggage camel has very powerful jaws, fitted with strong teeth. The number of teeth varies with the age of the camel. Most ruminants have cutting teeth on the lower jaw only, which bite against a pad on the upper jaw. The camel, however, has cutting teeth in both jaws. Hairs sprout from his long upper lip, which is cleft like a rabbit's. He uses it to feel, and sometimes to hold his food.

When he eats more food than he requires for his activities, some of it is stored in his hump in the form of fat. The hump, though it has no bone in it, then becomes solid and upright. At the end of a long period of starvation it shrinks to a mere drooping bag of skin. Many other animals store fat on the body—particularly those which hibernate, or are inactive, through the winter. The woodchuck, for instance, is plump when he retires to his hole in the autumn, and scrawny when he makes his spring appearance. Usually the fat is distributed over the body instead of concentrated in one spot, as it is in the camel's hump.

The camel is well fitted for life in the desert. His slanting slits of nostrils are lined

with hair and can be closed tight when a whirling sandstorm is raging. His big dark eyes, set far back on the sides of his head, are shielded from blowing grit and the sun's burning glare by a double fringe of long lashes, which interlock when the lids are

closed. The eye is further protected by an inner third eyelid. This thin membrane winks across the pupil to cleanse it of dust. His small, somewhat rounded ears are lined with hair. So well prepared is he for the assaults of wind-blown sand that even the sides of his longish tufted tail are fringed with hair that guards the bare skin beneath.

The coat of coarse hair which covers much of his body is short, but he has patches of longer, almost wool-like hair on his head, neck, throat, and hump, and often on the upper part of his forelegs. The color may range from white to black, but shades of sandy brown are the most common. Camels are always a single color; they are never striped or spotted.

The bare spots on the chest and on the joints of the long legs are present on all camels. They look as though the hair had worn off, but actually they are a natural condition. Even a baby camel soon shows these bald spots, but when he is about five months old the skin covering them becomes tough.

These horny callous pads act as shock absorbers, hitting the ground when the camel

suddenly drops to a kneeling position to rest. He goes down with front legs bent first and then folds his hind legs. Sometimes, when he is sleeping, he lies on his side. When he gets up, his movements are reversed; he jerks his hind legs up before straightening the front ones.

All his movements are accompanied by much squealing, grunting, and grumbling.

He is a noisy creature, protesting with or without reason. His strong smell is unpleasant, and few people have a kind word to say for his disposition. With his chin in the air, he wears an expression of haughty indifference. But his apparent disdain sometimes takes an unwelcome turn, when, without provocation, he will give a swift kick or dangerous bite. A known biter is often muzzled. When a camel is annoyed, he may suddenly spit, with good aim, shooting out a mouthful of slimy, ill-smelling cud at his victim.

At mating time, the male camel is apt to become very savage. Unlike deer, goats, and many other ruminants, he has no horns to use as weapons, so he uses his sharp teeth when fighting other males. He blows out a peculiar bladder from the side of his mouth and makes loud bubbling roars. During this period, unless he is securely tied, he is likely to attack anyone who ventures near him.

It is possible that a camel born in a zoo may be friendly, but as a work animal he shows no affection for the man who has charge of him, or even any recognition.

From the camel's point of view, however, this indifference is perhaps justified, because generations of these long-suffering enslaved animals have received harsh treatment from their owners. The camel is stubborn, but more likely than not he is right when he refuses to get up if he is tired, or seems to feel that he has been loaded too heavily.

The baggage camel usually carries from three to five hundred pounds. For a short trip, though, he may be loaded with six hundred pounds of freight. Any load must be balanced with great care. When at last he is on his way he walks at the rate of two to

three miles per hour and can travel about
thirty miles a day.

His manner of walking is called pacing, a
gait which causes him to rock along with a
jolting roll. He uses his legs in an odd way.
First he moves both legs on one side for-
ward at the same time. Then he does the
same thing with the legs on the other side.
This pacing gait is also used by some other
animals, among them bears, giraffes, and
newborn colts. Some people think that the
camel's nickname, ship of the desert, came
from his rolling walk. Others think of him

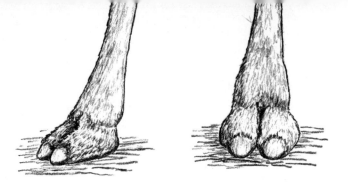

as a ship carrying freight across an ocean of sand.

The baggage camel's feet are built in a way that ensures excellent traction on yielding ground. Together with other camels, this Arabian, one-humped camel is classed by zoologists as an even-toed mammal. He is called a mammal, because, as a baby, he lived on his mother's milk; and he is known as even-toed, because he has an even number of toes (two of equal size) on each foot. He has hoofs, but each is like a comparatively small toenail on the toe's tip. Many

hoofed animals, such as the American buf-
falo, walk directly on the hoofs, but the
camel's weight rests on a broad pad which
connects the two long toes. Acting as an
elastic cushion, this base spreads when his
weight is on it, and supports him on loose
soil in the same way that a snowshoe keeps
its wearer on the top of the snow. When
the camel walks, his footsteps make no
sound.

An Arabian-camel mother has only one baby at a time. It is born eleven to twelve months after the mating of the parents. The woolly-coated baby can stand up on the day of his birth, but he is quite feeble; it takes a week for him to gain strength enough to run around. At about the end of a month, he begins to graze, but he also continues to get milk from his mother for some time. He shares the milk with the camel's owner.

If the herd is on the move, the new baby is slung in a net on the back of another camel and the mother follows it. If she carried the baby on her own back she would not know where it was and would wander disconsolately, looking for it.

When he is a few months old, the young baggage camel begins his training. He learns to accept a blanket tied over his back, and to stand and kneel on command. He learns to hold a kneeling position by having a cloth weighted with stones thrown over his back. But he never learns to enjoy taking orders. One nostril is pierced. This is done so that a ring or stud can be inserted for use when a rope is to be attached. This rope

may be used by the man who is leading him or it may be fastened to a strap under another camel's tail. Sometimes he is led by a rope tied to a strap secured around his jaws.

Having become accustomed to carrying a packsaddle and a gradually increased load, the young camel, at the age of about six years, begins to work as a baggage carrier. He is not fully grown until he is about sixteen years old, when he will have reached a height of six to seven feet at the shoulder. He may live to be about forty years old.

Many varieties of one-humped, or Arabian camels are used as baggage carriers in North Africa, the Middle East, India, Pakistan, and other countries. They thrive in parts of Australia, whose climate is suitable for them.

In many places a camel helps a farmer to draw water or harvest grain. Sometimes, instead of carrying a load on his back, he may be hitched to a cart filled, perhaps, with sixteen hundred pounds of freight.

More than a hundred years ago, camels
were brought to the United States for use
at frontier garrisons, but the experiment was
not a lasting success. In desert warfare else-
where, they have been indispensable as carriers of supplies, making their way through
country where no other means of transport
is possible.

The second type of Arabian, or one-
humped camel is used for riding.

Riding camels are bred with the greatest
care, and there are a number of recognized

varieties. They have many of the baggage camel's habits and characteristics but are longer-legged and less sturdily built. The riding camel, which walks, trots, canters, and gallops, can travel eighty miles a day at a very much faster rate than the plodding baggage camel. Over good ground, a racer can gallop

up to thirty-two miles per hour for a short
distance. He is guided by a single rein, and
the pressure of the rider's foot or stick on
his neck.

The riding saddle is a fitted wooden frame
padded with stuffed bags, often made of
camel leather. Frequently it is draped with

ornamental cloths, and the camel's head-gear is hung with tassels and bells. Women sometimes travel in a kind of tent set across the saddle.

In many wars, corps of fighting men have used specially trained dromedaries. The dromedary that Napoleon rode during his Egyptian campaign was afterward taken to France, where it lived in a menagerie. When it died its stuffed skin was exhibited in a museum, together with its saddle and em-broidered saddlecloth.

The Bactrian camel has two humps on his back, one behind the other. He gets his name from a country in Central Asia which was known as Bactria in ancient times. This camel is more heavily built than his Arabian cousins. His shorter legs and somewhat smaller, harder feet make it possible for him to travel safely over rough ground and up steep hillsides.

For part of the year he has a very thick coat of shaggy hair. This protection fits him for living in places where winters are cold and heavy snowstorms frequent. In the spring, he sheds the long hair from much of his body. It comes off in patches, giving him a shabby moth-eaten appearance.

Like all camels, the Bactrian species has many other uses besides being ridden and carrying baggage. The female's thick, rich

milk is an important food. Camel meat can be eaten. Camel hair is spun and woven into cloth for rugs, clothing, and tents, and made into rope. The skin is used to make boots, water containers, and all sorts of leather articles. Even camel droppings are valuable, for they are dried and used for fuel. The bones are extremely hard, and in some regions are used in place of ivory. Occasionally you can find pieces of camel bones in pet shops. They are sold for puppies to chew.

The Bactrian camel is not fussy about his food. He enjoys bitter plants which almost all other animals leave untouched. When pressed by hunger, he will eat whatever he can find—from felt blankets to fish. He likes salt and will drink the brackish water of salt lakes. Except for drinking purposes, he does not care for water and is a very poor swimmer.

At first, a baby Bactrian camel barely shows the humps that will have developed by the time he is two years old. The unborn baby is carried inside its mother for about thirteen months.

Both Bactrian and Arabian camels are used in some Asian regions, and occasionally the animals are crossbred. These mixed breed camels have the two humps of the Bactrian camel and the long legs of the Arabian.

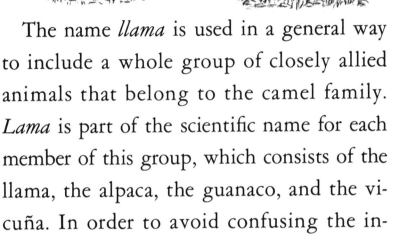

The name *llama* is used in a general way to include a whole group of closely allied animals that belong to the camel family. *Lama* is part of the scientific name for each member of this group, which consists of the llama, the alpaca, the guanaco, and the vicuña. In order to avoid confusing the individual animal called the llama with others of the tribe, the entire clan is sometimes known as the "lamoids."

Like the camel, each of the lamoids is a ruminant and has a chambered stomach, but unlike the camel, none of them has a hump for the storage of fat. Most have callous patches on the legs, though not as many as the camel. All have a woolly fleece. Actually, its fiber in a way resembles wool, which has cells in it that make it springy, and in a way, hair, which is not elastic.

The llama, a domesticated animal, is thought to be a descendant of the wild guanaco. He inhabits the high plateaus of the Andes, the mountain system that runs the length of western South America.

In the Peruvian Andes, and in parts of the Bolivian, the llama serves his owner as a burden bearer in much the same way as camels serve in their parts of the world.

Today's llama comes from a long line of

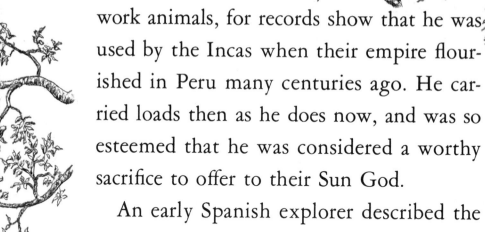

work animals, for records show that he was used by the Incas when their empire flourished in Peru many centuries ago. He carried loads then as he does now, and was so esteemed that he was considered a worthy sacrifice to offer to their Sun God.

An early Spanish explorer described the llama as a kind of camel-sheep, evidently noticing that the long-necked animal which carried its head so high resembled the camel even though it was much smaller. The llama is only distantly related to the sheep tribe. He is an even-toed hoofed ruminant, so he fits into the same order of mammals as sheep.

The llama's two-hoofed foot is narrow, with the hoofs pointed and slightly hooked. The toes have padded soles, but they are not joined as completely as in the camel's foot. The llama's type of foot fits him for scrambling along rocky trails and up steep mountain paths in an extraordinary sure-footed way.

The weight of a fully grown llama averages two hundred pounds—only a small fraction of the camel's. A big male llama may be about four feet high at the shoulder. The female is smaller. The llama's ears are relatively much longer than the camel's, and his bushy tail, carried crooked away from his body, is much shorter.

When the llama is working, he travels from twelve to fifteen miles a day. He carries a load of sixty pounds on a long, difficult trip. On an easier journey, an exceptional llama may pack as much as one hundred and thirty pounds. Only the male works, and he begins when he is three years old.

When he is traveling, the llama is given regular rest periods. Because he will not eat at night, he is given time to graze the herbage he finds along the way. Like the camel, he can get along without water for several days.

The llama is at home in the thin air and extreme cold of high mountains and thrives there. His thick woolly coat protects him from icy winds and snow. In color it varies from white to almost black, and often a light tone is blotched with darker spots.

His springy coat acts as a packsaddle, on which sacks of potatoes or other merchandise are carried, secured with soft ropes that go over his back and under his belly. He will not budge if he is tired or seems to feel he has been asked to carry too much. Nor will he allow himself to be harnessed to a cart.

Unlike the noisily protesting camel, the llama is usually a quiet creature. But like

the camel, he can kick and spit. In a zoo, a caged llama has been known to attract attention and disgust by aiming a mouthful of smelly liquid at a visitor.

The native Indian's herd of llamas is of great value to him. He treats them with the utmost kindness, never beating or even shouting at them to urge them on their way. He doesn't need to, because his gently trained llamas respond to a low whistle.

As many as five hundred llamas may travel together on a three weeks' trip. Usually moving along in single file, they follow

their leader, who is chosen for his ability
to pick the best way along the edge of a
precipice. He wears a bell and perhaps a
small flag on his head, or a tuft of colored
wool tied to each ear. These colored tassels,
or occasionally a dab of color on the fleece,
are also used as distinguishing marks of
ownership. At festival time, a favorite llama
is gaily decorated with bells and colored
streamers.

Only one fawn at a time is borne by a mother llama. Never used as a pack animal, she is kept for breeding purposes and for her fleece. Often Indian children make pets of baby llamas. Children also watch over resting herds grazing in sight of snow-capped mountain peaks.

Every bit of the llama, like every bit of
the camel, is useful to his owner. The rather
coarse woolly hair is spun and woven to
make his clothes and his ropes. The hide
furnishes leather for his sandals. The meat
is used for food. When the flesh is sliced
thin and dried in the sun, it is known as
charqui or, in English, jerky. The llama's
fat is used in the making of candles. His
dried droppings are valuable fuel, which,
before the coming of railroads, was the only
source of heat in the treeless regions.

Accounts of the alpaca as a domesticated
animal go as far back as the llama's records.
He, too, is believed to have descended from
the guanaco. Seldom more than three and a

half feet tall, he is rather smaller than the average llama, but slightly larger than the guanaco. He carries his tail close to his hindquarters and has a bulky, somewhat sheeplike appearance. Unlike other lamoids, he seldom has callous patches on his legs.

The alpaca's wool is finer than that of the

llama and is of greater length. Sometimes tangled strands reach almost to the ground. He is greatly prized for this oily fleece, which has no coarse outer hairs. In color, it is much like that of the llama. Black, brown, or spotted animals are commoner than the prized white ones. The alpaca's coat keeps him warm when the herds graze, sometimes in the company of llamas, on a cold plateau perhaps two and a half miles above sea level.

The alpaca is sheared every second year and yields about six pounds of wool. Because it is soft and shining, strong, warm, and light in weight, and because it sheds rain and snow easily, cloth made of this wool is in great demand. For commercial use, it is frequently mixed with other kinds of yarn.

The female alpaca gives birth to one baby at a time. Alpacas may live to be seven or more years old.

The guanaco is a wild animal. He is very much more rare now than in the past, but he has a wider range than the other lamoids. He is still found in the lofty valleys of the northern Andes, though he is more at home in the southern regions, such as the plains of Patagonia and Tierra del Fuego.

Living in herds of perhaps a hundred animals, the guanacos are wanderers. Each group is led by an old male. The guanaco is not as tall as the llama. He has a small head with long pointed ears, and his bushy tail is a mere stump. Usually his hair is dark reddish-brown on the upper parts of the body, and paler on the lower parts. The coarse fleece is not valued highly, but the meat is

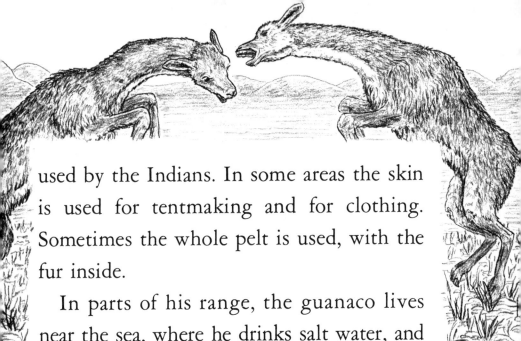

used by the Indians. In some areas the skin is used for tentmaking and for clothing. Sometimes the whole pelt is used, with the fur inside.

In parts of his range, the guanaco lives near the sea, where he drinks salt water, and swims well. He also has the habit of taking dust baths.

In the pairing season, male guanacos fight each other, biting fiercely and making a whinnying kind of cry. The mother guanaco nurses her new baby for about six weeks; then it begins to graze as well as suckle. At the end of three months, it is independent.

Less than three feet high at the shoulder, the vicuña is the smallest and rarest of the lamoids. He is a graceful creature somewhat like a deer, and yet in spite of his delicacy of build he is so hardy that he is able to live almost at the snow line of high mountains.

Domestication of the vicuña has not been altogether successful, for he seems to thrive best as a truly wild animal. Under government protection, vicuñas are now increasing in numbers. At one time they were in danger of becoming extinct, because they were hunted ceaselessly for the sake of their fleeces.

In color, the vicuña is cinnamon brown above, shading to yellowish beneath. The breast and belly are white.

There is no other wool so fine, so soft and silky—or so expensive to buy. It is so light that, when the vicuña is sheared, once a year, the entire fleece may weigh no more than eight ounces. It takes the cleaned wool from ten to twelve vicuñas to produce one yard of overcoat cloth.

Vicuñas live in small herds of six to fifteen females and one male. They are shy animals, as agile as an antelope when they go leaping away from suspected danger.

Usually a mother vicuña has but one baby at a time, although, very rarely, twins are born. The baby is active soon after its birth. Its short wool is soft as thistledown. Sometimes caught and raised by an Indian family, a baby fawn becomes a treasured, affectionate pet.

Some day, gasoline may replace camel power entirely—and synthetic fibers may take the place of animal wool. But until then man has many reasons to be grateful for camels and their relatives in the New World.